P9-CRX-155

BOOK SOLD
NO LONGER R.H.P.L
PROPERTY

CODE ACADEMY

Memory Madness!

By Kirsty Holmes

CRABTREE
PUBLISHING COMPANY
WWW.CRABTREEBOOKS.COM

CRABTREE
PUBLISHING COMPANY
WWW.CRABTREEBOOKS.COM

Author:
Kirsty Holmes
Editorial director:
Kathy Middleton
Editors:
John Wood, Crystal Sikkens
Proofreader:
Melissa Boyce
Graphic design:
Danielle Rippengill
Prepress technician:
Margaret Amy Salter
Print coordinator:
Katherine Berti

All images are courtesy of Shutterstock.com, unless otherwise specified. With thanks to Getty Images, Thinkstock Photo and iStockphoto.

Front Cover: kravik93, Incomible, Gelpi, Jag_cz, Nomad_Soul, Levent Konuk.

Interior: Background – teinstud. Characters: Ashwin – espies. Bailey – kravik93. Frankie – Kamira. Jia – PR Image Factory. Professor Chip – Elnur. Simon – YuryImaging. Sophia – MillaF. Ro-Bud – Carsten Reisinger. 5 – Iasha. 6 – MicroOne. 12 – ByEmo. 13 – Dzianis_Rakhuba, Ksander, Africa Studio. 17 – Nikolaeva. 18 – 0beron, SS1001, konzeptm, VectorShow. 20 – VVadyab Pico, Maksim M.

All facts, statistics, web addresses, and URLs in this book were verified as valid and accurate at time of writing. No responsibility for any changes to external websites or references can be accepted by either the author or publisher.

Some lines of code used in this book have been constructed for comedic purposes, and are not intended to represent working code.

Library and Archives Canada Cataloguing in Publication

Title: Memory madness! / Kirsty Holmes.
Names: Holmes, Kirsty, author.
Description: Series statement: Code Academy | Includes index.
Identifiers: Canadiana (print) 20190099054 |
  Canadiana (ebook) 20190099062 |
  ISBN 9780778763420 (softcover) |
  ISBN 9780778763369 (hardcover) |
  ISBN 9781427123404 (HTML)
Subjects: LCSH: Computer storage devices—Juvenile literature. |
  LCSH: Memory management (Computer   science)—Juvenile literature. |
  LCSH: Computer programming—Juvenile literature.
Classification: LCC TK7895.M4 H65 2019 | DDC j004.5—dc23

Library of Congress Cataloging-in-Publication Data

Names: Holmes, Kirsty, author.
Title: Memory madness! / Kirsty Holmes.
Description: New York, New York : Crabtree Publishing, [2019] | Series: Code academy | Audience: Ages: 5-7. | Audience: Grades: K-3. | Includes index.
  | Identifiers: LCCN 2019014258 (print) | LCCN 2019018676 (ebook) |
  ISBN 9781427123404 (Electronic) |
  ISBN 9780778763369 (hardcover) |
  ISBN 9780778763420 (pbk.)
Subjects: LCSH: Computer storage devices--Juvenile literature. | Computer programming--Juvenile literature.
Classification: LCC TK7895.M4 (ebook) | LCC TK7895.M4 .H65 2019 (print) |
  DDC 004.5--dc23
LC record available at https://lccn.loc.gov/2019014258

Crabtree Publishing Company

www.crabtreebooks.com   1–800–387–7650
Published by Crabtree Publishing Company in 2020
© 2019 BookLife Publishing Ltd.

All rights reserved. No part of this publication may be reproduced, stored in a retrieval system or be transmitted in any form or by any means, electronic, mechanical, photocopying, recording, or otherwise, without the prior written permission of Crabtree Publishing Company.

Printed in the U.S.A./072019/CG20190501

Published in Canada
Crabtree Publishing
616 Welland Ave.
St. Catharines, Ontario
L2M 5V6

Published in the United States
Crabtree Publishing
PMB 59051
350 Fifth Avenue, 59th Floor
New York, New York 10118

RICHMOND HILL PUBLIC LIBRARY
3297200 1544008   RV
Memory madness!
Sep. 10, 2019

CONTENTS

Hi, I'm Finn and this is Ava. Welcome to the world of coding! In this book you will learn the basics of computers and coding.

Words in bold, like **this**, can be found in the glossary on page 24.

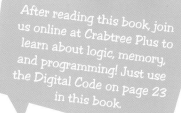

After reading this book, join us online at *Crabtree Plus* to learn about logic, memory, and programming! Just use the Digital Code on page 23 in this book.

ATTENDANCE

Code Academy is a school especially for kids who love computers and robots. Time to take attendance! Meet Class 101.

Simon

Sophia

Frankie

Jia

Ashwin

Bailey

Another day at Code Academy has begun. Today's lessons are about **memory**. Memory in a computer is where information is stored. The class will find out the answers to these questions:

- What is RAM?
- What is ROM?
- What is a byte?
- What is a backup copy?

Do I hear the bell...?

Ro-Bud

The students' robot classmate

MORNING LESSON

The students at Code Academy are putting on a school play. Everyone has their costumes and knows their lines. This afternoon is the first **performance**.

(2B) OR (!2B) = the_Question...?

HAMLET

Everyone has a part in the play.
Professor Chip is keeping everyone calm.

Two hours to go!

LUNCHTIME!

At lunchtime, everyone practices their lines. There is a lot to remember! It's really important to get them all right.

Ro-Bud is supposed to speak next, but she cannot remember her lines! Bailey is surprised. He is sure he saved Ro-Bud's lines in her memory.

The show cannot start! Ro-Bud has forgotten all her lines!

SHOW CANCELED!

Bailey's Fact:

This sounds like a memory problem. Let's take a look and see what is wrong.

11

GETTING HELP

Professor Chip knows there isn't much time!

There must be a problem with Ro-Bud's **storage systems**. Let's look it up.

MEMORY & STORAGE

Computers can hold a lot of **data**. Ro-Bud can store more information in her memory than a person can. She can remember things such as:

Photographs

Books

Music

Numbers

BAILEY BRINGS IT BACK

There are two main kinds of memory in a computer. The first one is called ROM. Its full name is Read-Only Memory. This is where **permanent** information that you always need to keep is stored.

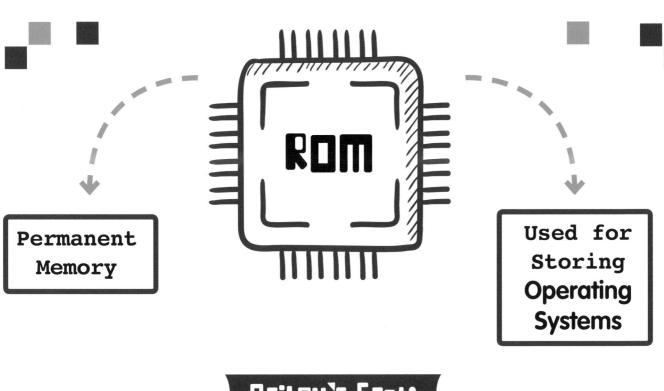

Permanent Memory

ROM

Used for Storing **Operating Systems**

Bailey's Fact:

Permanent information is still stored even when the computer is turned off.

How do you remember how to run, jump, and talk? Do you even think about it? No, you just remember how to do these things every time. If you were a computer, this type of memory would be your ROM.

The other type of memory is called RAM. Its full name is Random Access Memory. RAM is where new information or information you might only need for a while is stored. The information can be **deleted** when you no longer need it.

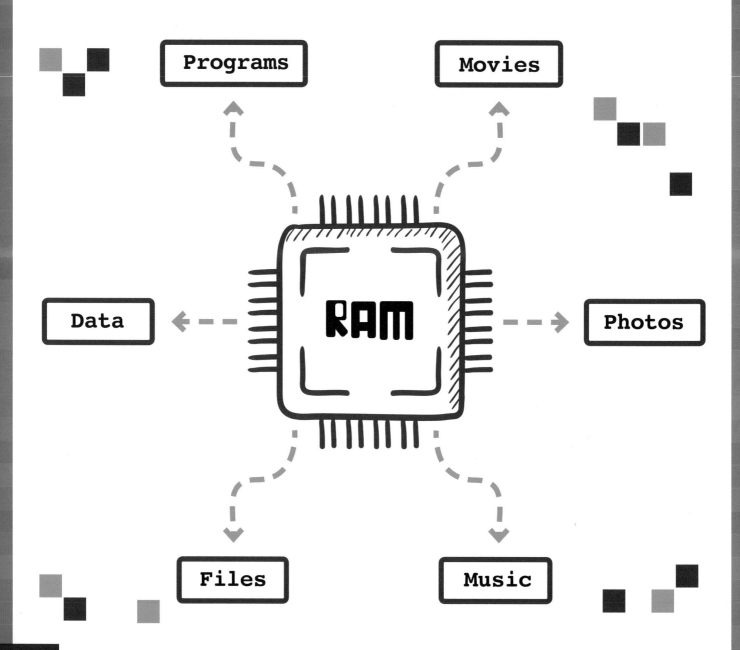

Imagine you are going to a music camp for a day. You learn the names of the other kids there. Your brain will have to find this information quickly all day long.

But you will not see these kids again after the camp is over. At the end of the day, this information can be forgotten. RAM stores information on a computer in the same way.

Ashwin's Fact:

Data on the RAM can be found easily. The data is deleted when the computer is turned off.

MEMORY MAGIC

So, how can Ro-Bud save her lines if they are stored on RAM memory? Ro-Bud can put the information on a storage system that is not part of her computer. This way, her lines do not get deleted when she shuts down. Here are some examples of storage systems.

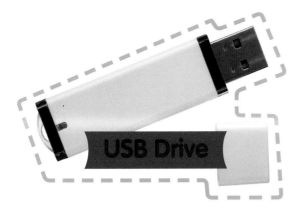

USB Drive

Cloud Storage

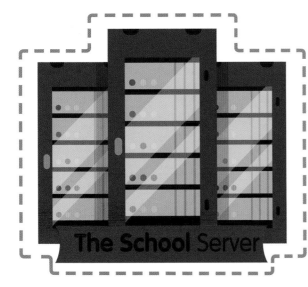

The School Server

Hard Disk Drive

Each type of storage holds a different amount of information. A **USB** drive can hold a small amount of information, such as homework. A bigger drive might be needed to store things like music or photos.

AMOUNT OF STORAGE SPACE	EXAMPLE OF WHAT CAN BE STORED
Byte	One letter of the alphabet
Kilobyte (KB)	Half a page of writing
Megabyte (MB)	4 books
Gigabyte (GB)	4,000 books
Terabyte (TB)	4,000,000 books

Today's smartphone has more memory than the first spacecraft that went to the Moon!

The computer's memory is like a big filing cabinet. It holds many different folders. Each folder holds pages of different information. The computer shows you the path to take to find where your file is saved.

FILE PATH: A file path tells you the order of folders to look in to get to your file. It is kind of like an address.

C>Class_101>Class_Projects>School_Play>Ro-Bud's_Lines

FILE TREE: This is a picture that shows the folders to follow to get to your file. Give your folders names that tell you what is in them. The folder at the top is called the parent folder. Folders inside this one are called child folders, or subfolders.

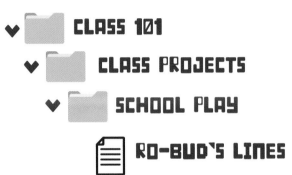

CLASS 101

CLASS PROJECTS

SCHOOL PLAY

RO-BUD'S LINES

FILENAME: This is the name of your computer file. A file is also called a document.

RO-BUD'S LINES

Always make a copy of an important file in case it gets lost. This copy is called a backup.

This is what the computer will show you
when you search for Ro-Bud's lines.

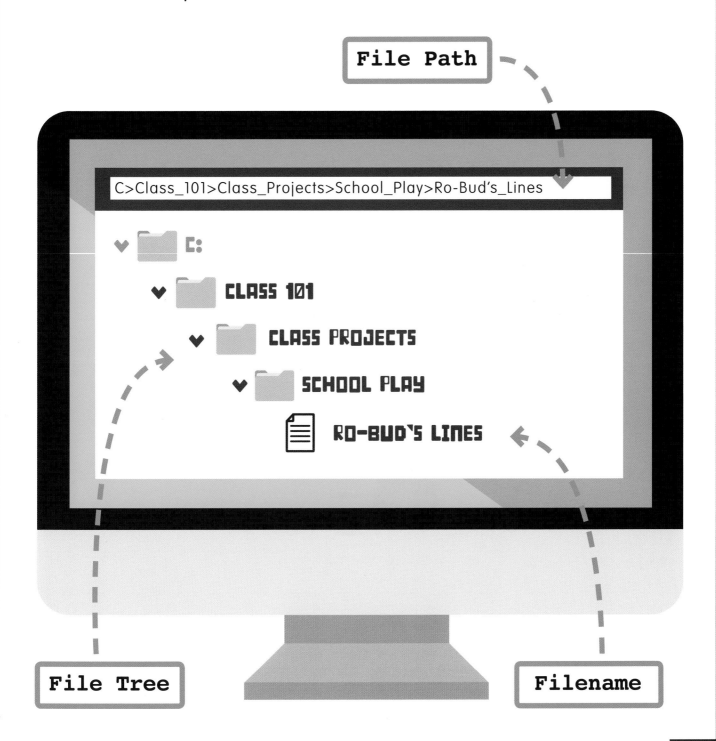

File Path

C>Class_101>Class_Projects>School_Play>Ro-Bud's_Lines

C:

CLASS 101

CLASS PROJECTS

SCHOOL PLAY

RO-BUD'S LINES

File Tree

Filename

21

SORTED OUT

Ro-Bud must have deleted her lines when she went to sleep. Don't worry! I made a backup copy and saved it on the **cloud**. Ro-bud, get ready to receive your lines.

LOOK IT UP

GLOSSARY:

cloud	The large computers that you can connect to and use for storing data on the Internet
data	Information
deleted	Permanently removed or erased
memory	Where information is stored in a computer
operating systems	Programs that control a computer
performance	A public presentation of something, such as a play
permanent	Meant to last for a very long time
server	A network of computers, for example in a school or business
storage systems	The parts of a computer that store information
USB	Universal Serial Bus, a type of connector for computers

INDEX: